Joy

Fruit of the Spirit

JOY

YOUR DAILY MEDITATION

SISTER IRINI

Bible references (*Italics*): New Revised Standard Version Updated Edition (NRSVUE) from bible gateway.com

Cover Design: Lovo.Ai Virtual Art
Editing: Chat GPT 4
ISBN: 978-1-7386223-6-8

SEASEM PUBLICATIONS
publications@seasem.org

I have said these things to you so that my joy may be in you and that your joy may be complete.

John 15:11

Contents

Introduction

Have you ever felt a sense of joy so profound that its radiance seemed to fill every fibre of your being? A joy so deep and abiding that nothing could shake it?

Radiant joy is a gift from God, a divine grace that emanates from the luminosity of your soul. It is not something you earn or deserve through your own efforts. It doesn't come from simply being and doing good or experiencing delightful things. It is a direct translation of your relationship with Jesus Christ and the work of the Holy Spirit in you that by your faith God births joy. It is a fruit of the Spirit quite literally born out of your spiritual growth in Jesus Christ.

Joy as a fruit of the Spirit is not a fleeting emotion subject to fluctuations that ripple with your mood according to external or internal cognitive or other physiological stimuli. You will have all the range of emotions and still live with all that the Holy Spirit has clarified within you to produce this wondrous joy. You could be sick, have moments of frustration, experience fear and all the natural passions of needing to eat and drink, sleep, desire friendship or community and companionship. You may feel sad at times or have bursts of world inspired joy as when a darling new born takes a first breath. All of these natural feelings and reaching occur while remaining in relationship with God. They have no bearing on the Lord's grace that is joy.

God's joy is gratifying even when it is confession and repentance preceding forgiveness, atonement and liberation. Yes, the fruit of joy boldly steps into the place of doubt, of despondency, uncertainty, of emotion and material loss or gain.

The fruit of the Spirit that is divine joy is overcoming the cross. It is the joy of Jesus knowing his life, crucifixion, death and resurrection secures humanity's eternal life. Imagine that joy. It comes from a place of deep and abiding love. Love of God the Almighty. Love of humanity. That joy comes from a selflessness that wants to raise another up, wants to give life to all. It is a ceaseless joy. Obedient to God. By its very nature, that joy is self-rewarding, and the overflow of God's blessing in that joy, blesses others.

Because of its divine origins that joy is creative. It has the capacity to create change in the world. To uplift, to alter, to magnify, to reveal, to heal, to bless–you and others. And, even as you live that joy, you glorify God in doing so. That is the fruit of the Spirit that is divine joy.

Fruit of the Spirit

Each one of us is called to love, joy, peace, patience, kindness, generosity, faithfulness, gentleness, and self-control (Galatians 5:22-23). These are the fruit of the Spirit; positive outcomes of living true to the Spirit of God inside us. But what are they and how can we actively live out the fruit of the Spirit in our daily lives?

Beyond Everyday Virtues

At the heart of this series of meditation books is the understanding that the fruit of the Spirit are not simply ethical behaviours or moral goals. They are the manifestations of the Holy Spirit's work within us that transforms us into the likeness of Jesus Christ. Unlike virtues we might strive for through our own efforts, these fruit are a grace, a gift from God that deepens our relationship with God. They are divine energies that assist us to 'become participants of the divine nature.' (2 Peter 1:4)

Divine Energies

Divine energies are the way God reveals God's self in the world. Unlike the essence of God, which is beyond our comprehension, divine energies allow us to experience God's presence and action in our lives. These energies are uncreated, timeless and eternal, flowing from God's being, within us and about us, drawing us closer to God and to our true selves.

Living the Fruit

The fruit of the Spirit are direct outcomes of our proximity to God inside us. The more available to the Spirit we become, the more the divine energies of the Holy Spirit transform us. This book offers you thirty days of bathing in those energies. Through daily meditations on scripture, prayer and practical exercise, you spend time with God, creating rich soil that enable the Holy Spirit to transform your life. The personal revelation you receive will enhance how you relate to God, with others and yourself. By opening to the Spirit of God this way, your life will positively change as your soul's light increasingly reflects the divinity inside you.

Fruitful Change

Read how these meditations on the Word of God have been blessing people.

Betty's Renewal Betty found the meditations simple yet profoundly beautiful. The experience inspired her to travel to America from Australia for Easter to join her favourite preacher's ministry. The fruit of faithfulness, empowered by God's love and Word provided for Betty's dreams. And the fruit of Love has helped her branch out into Christian community and fellowship in a new way.

Tracy's Open Heart Tracy and her husband faced repeated tension in their marriage. The meditations helped 're-centre' Tracy to open her heart to her husband. He responded favourably, and almost instantly their relationship was transformed. The peace of Christ strengthened their love and entered their ongoing communication.

Angela's Patience Through the daily mediations, Angela realised that patience was absent in her upbringing, affecting her relationships. This revelation, fuelled by the power of the Holy Spirit, birthed the fruit of patience in Angela. Out of this revelation, faith and courage grew in her, and family relations were mended and deepened.

Anita's Conviction: Coming from a New Age background, Anita found herself embracing the meditations but feeling resistant and fearful when invited to defend the gospel. A church reading on the Apostle Thomas confirmed her personal revelation through the Word that day. She saw the works of the Holy Spirit then reinforcing her faith journey and the joy of God entered her, overcoming any fear and doubt.

Kathleen's Direction: New to Jesus, Kathleen realised through the daily scripture and prayer that her calling lay beyond her chosen field of psychotherapy. Part way through the meditations she retired, declaring 'It wasn't right and I just needed to let it go.' Kathleen knew she was called to serve in a different way. As she embraced the Holy Spirit's work in her, her life was redirected towards a deepening of her relationship with God. Her faith was strengthened and she met the change with courage and conviction.

Siyu's Healing After a painful relationship ending, Siyu found solace in the daily meditations, experiencing the Word of God and God's love afresh: 'I'm trusting the healing process and trusting God.' By letting the Spirit lead her, Siyu encountered surprising conversations with strangers that gave her comfort and led her into new spiritual fellowship. Her Christian faith was lit as she declared trust in God who heals and restores.

These testimonies declare power of living and walking in the Spirit as we remain faithful to the true vine that is Jesus Christ. More than intellectual exercises; the daily mediations open us to the divine grace God wants to bestow upon our life.

What to Expect

When you embark upon these meditations, you can expect change. Expect spiritual and emotional growth, and a richer, deeper relationship with God inside you. Notice your increased empathy, compassion and forgiveness. Be aware of how your personal relationships are blessed, and how the way you connect with people in general changes.

Your speech will be more considered. There will be increased stillness and silence with a desire towards sincerity.

This beauty that is authenticity stems from the grace God bestows upon us as we turn more and more towards the uncreate light within us. You will notice this growing sense of authenticity as God invites you to be increasingly and unapologetically, simply yourself in the divine energies.

With this simplicity of truth comes a heightened sense of inner peace, a renewed motivation towards acts of kindness and service, and a shift in the way you view the world towards love and positivity. Nuances of change specific to your own life and personality will emerge. God's divine love will draw out of you the best of you, and free you from limitations you have in love. Be prepared to say yes to these changes. They may be unfamiliar at first but the rewards are sublime.

Divine Reading

Here's how to approach your meditation. Divine reading, known as *Lectio Divina*, invites you into a deeply contemplative engagement with scripture. This fourfold path will be the jewel of your meditation experience with God.

1. **Read** Approach the daily scripture as you would a dear friend—with an open heart. Slowly read the passage, reverently whispering it aloud multiple times.

2. **Meditate** Now, gently reflect on the passage. This is an almost peripheral state of consciousness rather than a piercing analysis. The passage floats in awareness inviting you to notice how it interacts with aspects of your life. Observe any feelings or emotions that arise here, letting

them rise and fall without following in thought too far.

3. **Pray** Pray the prayer provided or respond to the passage with your own prayer. Then ask God, 'What do you have for me?' Here, you are opening to personal revelation that is unique to you. Pray and listen for a response. Notice any imagery that appears or spontaneous realisations. You will know the Word of God by its interruption in your process, by the newness it brings, the growth it inspires, the 'flavour' of the thought being different to your everyday thinking and the command of it. Remember, God never criticises, bullies, or hurts. God will only ever illuminate, reveal, guide or lead you for your good.

4. **Contemplate** With your heart longing to be met, the Spirit of God will respond. Rest now in the presence of God, allowing any revelation to find home in your heart.

In sublime contemplation, the mind slips away, the body ceases to protect, the world quietens as you become a spiritual being. Tears may release the joy of your union with God. Commit to the invitation God gives you. You might give thanks now, ask Jesus for forgiveness, open to healing, praise God or simply rest in the divine presence.

Practice

This is where the fruit of the Spirit is lived and shared. Practical exercises are given, allowing God the great adventure of participating in you taking the divine illumination into the world. As part of your daily practice you may like to keep a journal. This is particularly helpful for remembering God's word to you and recording any insights into the application of the Word in your life.

Obstacles

Do not be alarmed if you encounter obstacles to your meditations. And remember that the daily rhythm is a guide only. Go at God's pace, which might not be daily. Here are some examples of potential obstacles:

1. **Mistaking Divine Reading for Bible Study** Being caught up in what words mean or scriptural context, keeps you in the head rather than the heart. Let go of study and biblical analysis for the heart to open to divine leading.

2. **Ignoring Life Context** Remember your life context. Be mindful of how the Bible passage relates to certain aspects of your life, and notice the feelings, thoughts and emotions that arise at this time.

3. **Being Cut Off from Emotions** It is important to acknowledge emotions, even the uncomfortable or painful ones. Without dwelling on them, notice how they add to your life context in relation to the scripture passage.

4. **Hurrying** Slow down. Divine reading is not a race but a contemplation. Trust in God's timing. Revelation may not happen in the meditation but days or even weeks later.

5. **Be Kind** How you know and experience God is unique to you. Be kind with yourself in the daily process. Give yourself every measure of harmonious support, even if you fall asleep! Sometimes God simply wants you to rest in the Spirit.

6. **Doubting and Skepticism** Of all the obstacles to God's grace, doubt and skepticism are the most damaging. 'Did I really hear that word?' 'Am I making it up?' 'Was it real?'

Scepticism immediately separates us from God in the moment. Any word God has for us is lost to doubt. Please, allow God, and if you have doubts, take them to a spiritual director or companion, pray on them again or check scripture for a precedent.

7. **Limiting God** It may be tempting to stop the meditations after one revelation. You received a word from God, and amazed by the insight in your life, you rest content in the meditative success. The Holy Spirit continues to do works in and for us. And we must say, 'Yes, here am I God.' The fruit of the Spirit is adventuring to make of your soul a permanent home for divine illumination and for the fruit of the Spirit. Let your prayer be, 'More, Holy Spirit, give me more!'

The Invitation

As you meet these meditations, trust that the Spirit of God within you—you in those glorious divine energies of the twice holy God—have prepared you to blossom as you open to the Holy Spirit's gift of joy. Anticipate the encounter you will have with those divine energies. Co-operate with them by sitting with an open heart and mind, becoming available to the grace God wants to bestow upon you. There is boundless delight on offer; fearless understanding, and heavenly possibilities for your life here and now. Joy upon joy.

May the light of all glories bless you and keep you. And may you, having put on the light of Christ, become its very illumination in the world.

Sister Irini

Joy

Your Daily Meditation

Day 1

Fruit of the Spirit

The fruit of the Spirit is love, joy, peace, forbearance,
kindness, goodness, faithfulness, gentleness,
and self-control.

Galatians 5:22-23

Prayer

O Lord, thank you for the fruit of the spirit that is joy. Help me to recognise and to feel this joy you give me. Amen.

Joyful Daily Practice

Take time for yourself today in silence. Feel yourself empty of worldly thoughts, as you turn to Jesus. Without effort or expectation, just let him know that you are here, open-hearted, available to his joy. Then, take note of your day.

Day 2

This is the Day

This is the day that the Lord has made;
let us rejoice and be glad in it.

Psalm 118:24

Prayer

I thank you God for the gift of today. Though it's not always easy to rejoice and to be glad Lord. I do rejoice in you Jesus. Thank you. Thank you. Let my heart be filled with you. Amen.

Joyful Daily Practice

Reflect on all that you are grateful for today from the perspective of your life being a precious, tender creation of a God Who loves you faithfully, eternally.

Day 3

Shout for Joy

The meadows are covered with flocks and the valleys are mantled with grain; they shout for joy and sing.

Psalm 65:13

Prayer

Heavenly Father, we rejoice in the abundance of your provision. Thank you for your faithful care that brings joy to our lives. May our hearts be filled with gratitude for your abundant blessings. Amen.

Joyful Daily Practice

Nature and the glory of God's creation in the natural world inspires us, uplifts and breathes the life of our Creator as we breathe. Walk in nature today. Skip or sing. Dance or laugh. Shout out or cry. Know that the abundance of life around you is a joyful creation of the hand Who holds you and nurtures you when you permit it.

Day 4

Rejoice in Hope

Rejoice in hope, be patient in tribulation, be constant in prayer.

Romans 12:12

Prayer

Lord, help us to find joy in the hope we have in you. Grant us patience in times of trial, and may our hearts remain steadfast in constant prayer. Amen.

Joyful Daily Practice

Focus on a specific hope you have in Christ today, and let it be a source of joy and encouragement in the midst of any challenges.

Day 5

Rejoice Always

Rejoice always,
pray without ceasing,
give thanks in all circumstances,
for this is the will of God in Christ Jesus for you.

1 Thessalonians 5:16-18

Prayer

Lord Jesus Christ, Son of God, have mercy on me.
Lord Jesus Christ, Son of God, have mercy on me.
Lord Jesus Christ, Son of God, have mercy on me. Amen.

Joyful Daily Practice

To pray this, the Jesus Prayer repeatedly throughout the day. Becoming aware of every blessing in your life. Being thankful for every condition, concerning every condition, and in every condition of your life.

Day 6

For the One Who Repents

Just so, I tell you, there will be more joy in heaven over one sinner who repents than over ninety-nine righteous persons who need no repentance.

Luke 15:7

Prayer

Heavenly Father, I declare with joy that you have done great things for me; that all my sins are forgiven through our Saviour, Lord Jesus Christ and that I am free in my heart to be truly, honestly, openly righteous in you. Amen.

Joyful Daily Practice

Pause to reflect on your courageous remorse for past errors and behaviours that separated you from God. Or if you need to repent you could attend confession with a spiritual director or priest or speak to Jesus and wait for His forgiveness. You may go to church and partake of the Holy Sacrament of the Eucharist for the forgiveness of your sins.

Day 7

Joy Comes

Weeping may linger for the night,
but joy comes with the morning.

Psalm 30:5

Prayer

In moments of sorrow, we trust in your promise God that joy will come in the morning. Thank you for your enduring favour and the assurance of your comforting presence. Amen.

Joyful Daily Practice

Know that tears do not linger in Christ. He will restore and uplift. Joy will replace sorrow. Consider a time in your life when this was so, and bathe in the light of that promise.

Day 8

Joy and Peace

May the God of hope fill you with all joy and peace in believing, so that you may abound in hope by the power of the Holy Spirit.

Romans 15:13

Prayer

Come Holy Spirit. Come. Saturate me in the peace of the Lord. Pour forth living faith, hope alive in you. Amen.

Joyful Daily Practice

Take time today to reflect on your faith in God. Notice how belief and hope become expectations in your conviction of faith. And how that certainty brings peace and joy. Set your faith to light up a particular situation in your life, knowing that it will bare good fruit by the power of the Holy Spirit.

Day 9

A Joyful Heart

A joyful heart is good medicine, but a crushed spirit dries up the bones.

Proverbs 17:22

Prayer

O Lord, accept my prayer this day and every day. Lord, grant us joyful hearts that bring healing and refreshment to our lives and the lives of others. Help us to cultivate joy even in challenging circumstances. Amen.

Joyful Daily Practice

Find humour in everyday situations, share a laugh with someone today, and let the joyous moment serve as medicine for your soul.

Day 10

Clothed in Joy

You have turned my mourning into dancing; you have taken off my sackcloth and clothed me with joy so that my soul may praise you and not be silent.

Psalm 30:11-12

Prayer

At times my pain has been so great Lord. Seemingly unendurable. But you God, you have brought me through. You have turned my mourning into dancing. Let this be so again, now and forever. Amen.

Joyful Daily Practice

Sometimes we suffer and carry unspeakable burdens of grief; grief that is personal, private or shared; grief that touches the core of our life. Through Jesus Christ that grief is changed. We are restored through Jesus. It is physical, emotional and spiritual. Feel the cloth of joy on you today, in a new way, and in your way, praise God.

Day 11

Look to Jesus

Looking to Jesus, the pioneer and perfecter of faith, who for the sake of the joy that was set before him endured the cross, disregarding its shame, and has taken his seat at the right hand of the throne of God.

Hebrews 12:2

Prayer

Jesus, I see your face, a perfect person. I stand before you humbled by your love and your sacrifice. I see your divinity and worship you. O Lord, make of me one who all persons see you in. Let your glory shine through me. Amen.

Joyful Daily Practice

Today, spend time seeking Christ in you through an image of Jesus. Let the icon or painting draw you closer to your Saviour so that you feel in your heart of hearts His presence.

Day 12

Praise Him

My heart leaps for joy, and with my song, I praise him.

Psalm 28:7

Prayer

You God are my strength and shield. I trust in you and find joy in your presence. Today, let my heart leap with joy as I praise you with my words of gratitude.

Joyful Daily Practice

Take a moment to dance or move joyfully. Allow the rhythm to lift your spirits and fill your heart with joy. Leap for joy outside or within your home. Sing, glorify. Magnify your love for Jesus through an open heart that rises to melody heard or felt within.

Day 13

Love Him

Although you have not seen him, you love him;
and even though you do not see him now,
you believe in him and and rejoice with an
indescribable and glorious joy.

1 Peter 1:8

Prayer

Lord Jesus, though we have not seen you, we love you, and though we do not see you now, we believe in you. Fill us with your inexpressible and glorious joy, a joy that surpasses all understanding. Amen.

Joyful Daily Practice

Reflect on the love of Christ and the hope of salvation, allowing it to fill you with joy that transcends circumstance, bringing peace to your heart.

Day 14

Joy of My Heart

Your decrees are my heritage forever;
they are the joy of my heart.

Psalm 119:111

Prayer

O Lord, I choose my inheritance in you. I choose access to Your Kingdom. I choose grace and life eternal always, ever over the world. Your decrees are my heritage. And You are the joy of my heart! Amen.

Joyful Daily Practice

Think on the spiritual benefits and eternal blessings that are yours as a believer. Feel the joy of that truth. Notice what that joy invites you into more deeply. Pay heed to it as an invitation of the Holy Spirit.

Day 15

Sing

Sing for joy, O heavens, and exult, O earth;
break forth, O mountains, into singing!
For the Lord has comforted his people
and will have compassion on his suffering ones.

Isaiah 49:13

Prayer

O gracious and merciful God, we join the heavens, earth and mountains in joyful praise. We rejoice for your comfort and compassion, for your mercy that brings joy to those in need and relief to those who suffer. Let [insert names of those in need] be comforted this hour. Amen.

Joyful Daily Practice

Find a moment today to praise God for His comfort and compassion. Consider a time when your pain was great, and your prayers of relief answered. Pray this blessing for yourself or others today. Let your faith in God's promises bring joy

Day 16

Leap for Joy

For as soon as I heard the sound of your greeting, the child in my womb leaped for joy.

Luke 1:44

Prayer

Mary, Mother of God, thank you for the gift of our Saviour Jesus Christ. Queen of Heaven, sinless by grace, example to us all. In your Son's name, Jesus Christ, we thank you. Amen.

Joyful Daily Practice

Consider the beauty, grace and love of motherhood. The loss in motherhood too. The unimaginable heartache and the magnificent love. Reflect on Mary, the Mother of Jesus and her faithfulness to God and to her son, Jesus Christ. What might her love and God's works in her offer you today?

Day 17

Fullness of Joy

You show me the path of life.
In your presence there is fullness of joy;
in your right hand are pleasures forevermore.
Psalm 16:11

Prayer

Gracious God, into your hands I commend my life. Through your handiwork, my path is revealed. May the eternal pleasures found at your right hand be a source of lasting joy and fulfilment in our lives. Amen.

Joyful Daily Practice

Set aside time for personal prayer and reflection, seeking God's guidance for your life. Notice where you may or may not be attending to God's will. As you experience His presence, allow the joy that comes from walking His path to resonate in your heart.

Day 18

He is Your Strength

The joy of the Lord is your strength.

Nehemiah 8:10b

Prayer

Jesus, thank you for being my source of joy and strength. Help me to find deeper joy in your presence and let it empower me in all that I do. Amen.

Joyful Daily Practice

Take a moment to reflect on something that you do with or for Jesus that brings you joy, and let it fill you with strength and positivity throughout the day. Consider too how you might expand that thing into new service, new behaviours, new prayer, new worship. Let God lead you in what that might be.

Day 19

Serve the Lord

Make a joyful noise to the Lord, all the earth.
Serve the Lord with gladness;
come into his presence with singing.

Psalm 100:1-2

Prayer

[Sing this prayer] Thank you Lord for the joy that fills my heart. I sing praises to you today O God. I praise you, I worship you, I thank you O God.

Joyful Daily Practice

Each morning this week, begin your day with a smile, consciously choosing joy. Sing to God. Even a few lines of praise; what is on your heart.

Day 20

With All Strength

May you be made strong with all the strength that comes from his glorious power, so that you may have all endurance and patience, joyfully giving thanks to the Father, who has enabled you to share in the inheritance of the saints in the light.

Colossians 1:11-12

Prayer

Heavenly Father, strengthen me with your glorious power, enabling me to endure with joyful patience all matters that come my way. Amen.

Joyful Daily Practice

Consider with gratitude the many ways you have been spiritually renewed living in God's truth and grace. Write about this today or share a story from your experience with someone.

Day 21

Endurance

My brothers and sisters, whenever you face various trials, consider it all joy,
because you know that the testing of your faith produces endurance.

James 1:2

Prayer

O merciful God, fill me with joy even as I face trials. When I am low and cannot find joy myself, in your mercy, let me know your joy Lord. Amen.

Joyful Daily Practice

Think of a trial you have been through or face now. You do not have to face it alone. Jesus Christ offers to stand with you. Though faith may be tested, still our steadfastness in Christ produces the very fruit we meditate upon here. Reflect on how your enduring faith has held you in good stead or if you are new to faith, think about this enduring promise God makes to you.

Day 22

A Willing Spirit

Restore to me the joy of your salvation,

and sustain in me a willing spirit.

Psalm 51:12

Prayer

Heavenly Father, in moments of repentance and reflection, restore to me the joy of your salvation. Grant me a willing spirit to do your will now and forever. Amen.

Joyful Daily Practice

Take time to reflect on your salvation journey. Consider the moments when you first experienced the joy of God's saving grace. Express gratitude for the ongoing work of salvation in your life and let this joy bubble up.

Day 23

Joy in the Holy Spirit

For the kingdom of God is not food and drink but righteousness and peace and joy in the Holy Spirit.

Romans 14:17

Prayer

Heavenly Father, help me to recognise the true essence of your kingdom. Fill my heart with the joy that surpasses worldly concerns, drawing me to you. Amen.

Joyful Daily Practice

Today, intentionally pursue righteousness, seek peace in your relationships, and embrace the joy that comes from the presence of the Holy Spirit. Allow these qualities to shape your interactions and mindset throughout the day.

Day 24

Shout for His Glory

But rejoice insofar as you are sharing Christ's sufferings, so that you may also be glad and shout for joy when his glory is revealed.

1 Peter 4:13

Prayer

Heavenly Father, fill my heart with Your strength and peace. Help me to seek not the fleeting comforts of the world but the deeper joy that comes from knowing You. Amen

Joyful Daily Practice

Take a walk and with each step, consider the suffering and life of Jesus, all the way through His crucifixion to His resurrection, and know that He loves you and is joyful for your life. Let that love and joy arise in you.

Day 25

No One Will Take Your Joy

So you have pain now, but I will see you again, and your hearts will rejoice, and no one will take your joy from you.

John 16:22

Prayer

O Lord, thank you for preparing a place for me. Thank you for taking me there. You are my joy and in you my joy is secure. I rejoice in you my God. Amen.

Joyful Daily Practice

This is the day to ponder everlasting joy. Your life continues beyond this physical life. Your joy now is incomparable with the joy to come. Let this sink in today. And give thanks. And know that the joy that awaits you can be brought into your life now. Heavenly realities are available on earth now. Through Jesus Christ, no one will take your joy from you.

Day 26

Glad by His Works

For you, O Lord, have made me glad by your work;
at the works of your hands I sing for joy.

Psalm 92:4

Prayer

O Lord, you bring me gladness. Your goodness and faithfulness is the handiwork by which my life is created. Your presence, your power, your might is my joy.

Joyful Daily Practice

What are the works of God's hand upon your life? Take a moment to open your heart to consider effort God goes to in order to care for you, to bring you closer, to ensure your joy. Consider this creativity, in the world too. Despite all the suffering, all of humanity's troubles and wrongdoings, open your heart to God's beauty today.

Day 27

Ask for Anything

Until now you have not asked for anything in my name. Ask and you will receive, so that your joy may be complete.

John 16:24

Prayer

Gracious Lord, teach me to seek You more boldly. Grant me to receive more completely; help me to ask more honestly, to know you more deeply, to trust fully in You that my joy may be complete. Amen.

Joyful Daily Practice

Open your heart today to Jesus. Feel the closeness of God within. Upon that nearness, ask that which is on your heart. Know in your heart of hearts that God's promises are real and true and Christ will grant you blessing that brings fruit. Let your servant's heart be glorified even as you glorify God.

Day 28

Exult in God

Though the fig tree does not blossom and no fruit is on the vines; though the produce of the olive fails and the fields yield no food; though the flock is cut off from the fold and there is no herd in the stalls, yet I will rejoice in the Lord; I will exult in the God of my salvation.

Habakkuk 3:17-18

Prayer

Through all things Lord, You are my salvation. Through the depth of my searching. Through the barrenness and sorrow; through the pain and grief; through the poverty and hardship, You God, remain my light and the hope in Whom I rejoice. Hallelujah!

Joyful Daily Practice

Find a way to express the bounty and abundance of God's hand upon your life today. Whether through creativity–a poem, a prayer, a song, a painting–or a testimony shared, a walk in nature and a joyful reflection, a Church reading or by giving in Christ's name.

Day 29

Sing for Joy

But let all who take refuge in You rejoice; let them ever sing for joy. Spread Your protection over them so that those who love Your name may exult You.

Psalm5:11

Prayer

O Lord, You are my refuge and my salvation. You envelope me in your mantle and projection. Shelter me in your love. You are my defender and my shield, my overcomer and conqueror of the world. In Your name I rise victorious in joy and in love. Amen

Joyful Daily Practice

Take a moment to feel God's protection over you and notice what arises in you, and whether it comforts in and of itself or it moves you to act in a God-given way.

Day 30

His Joy is in You

I have said these things to you so that my joy may be in you, and that your joy may be complete.

John 15:11

Prayer

O Lord, you are the Word, and your word lives within me. You, Who ever was and always will be, You are my joy, my heart and my life. Amen.

Joyful Daily Practice

Take time today to immerse in the word of God. Notice how it speaks into your life.

The Fruit of Joy

O how you have opened your heart to something remarkable in God's love that manifests joy. The grace you've encountered, the revelations received, the spiritual insights that have illuminated your path; they are not simply experiences for a passing season. They are invitations to an ongoing relationship that draws you ever closer to God's heart and to the divine nature that you share through your Christification—your becoming more and more Christ like.

Remember that joy, as a fruit of the Spirit, is not something that can be experienced once and forgotten. It is a living, active grace that continues to flourish as you remain open to the work of the Holy Spirit in you. Just as a seed planted in rich soil does not stop growing but reaches towards the sun, so too your joy will deepen, expand, and bear new fruit as you remain rooted in God and open to the works of the Spirit.

By walking through these daily reflections, the Holy Spirit has shaped aspects of your being. Each passage, each prayer whispered, and each act of love or kindness inspired by the readings has been an offering to God—a moment of surrender that has invited the Holy Spirit to dwell more fully in your life, growing you in virtue and in holiness.

Embracing Joy Beyond this Journey

Now, as you step beyond these meditations, consider how you will continue to cultivate that joy. The glory of spiritual growth is that it is ever-continuing; God's grace is limitless, and the joy found in God's presence can deepen beyond your imagination. Each day is an opportunity to walk in the Spirit, nourishing the seeds of joy planted in your heart.

Be mindful that this joy is not just for times of peace. True, Spirit-filled joy is a strength that endures, shines brightest, and radiates warmth even in the face of life's inevitable challenges. It is a joy that does not falter when storms arise but holds fast to God's promises and presence. When moments of trial and sorrow come, this joy will be your anchor, allowing you to live in the assurance that God is near and that God's love for you is unshakable.

Embrace the fruit of joy as a steadfast friend whom you can call on and rely on to rise up by grace, through your faith when you turn to it.

Continuing the Practice of Joy

Along with the Holy Sacraments that include partaking of the Eucharist, the Holy Communion, in remembrance of Jesus and for forgiveness of sin—those times we fall out of communion with God—it is helpful to keep the practices of meditation, prayer, and practical exercises as part of your spiritual life. Remember to create space in your day to sit quietly with God, to listen deeply for God's voice. Engage in divine reading, not just as a discipline, but as a cherished time of communion with the Lord.

Continue to enter nature and all that God has created for you. Love on your animal companions. Hug a tree. Walk a beach. Sit in wonder before a sunrise or a sunset. Bask beneath a star filled sky, and take in all of God's creation. *The heavens are telling the glory of God, and the firmament proclaims his handiwork.* (Psalm 19:1) God's splendour and handiwork, and the majesty of the Lord's most perfect creation may be perceived through the divine order of creation, as well as in our own lives. Give thanks in these places. Feel God's unique and special love just for you there in the nature of creation.

The small, practical acts of joy you have engaged in are not merely exercises but the embodiment of the fruit of the Spirit in your life. Continue to make space for these practices. Share your joy with others, let it spill over into your family, amongst your friends, in your church community, place of work, or your community in general. Allow the light of Christ within you to bring healing, encouragement, and love to those around you.

Remember, joy is the overflow of God's love in and for you, to be shared, witnessed to others, to bless, and to glorify God.

Rejoicing in God's Work in You

As you skip with the fruit of joy, take time to celebrate the changes and growth that have taken place in you. God has been at work in you—whether through gentle whispers, moments of conviction, or bursts of clarity that have shifted the way you see yourself and your world. Allow yourself to rejoice in this holy work, giving thanks for how Christ has shaped and renewed you.

When you live in the joy of the Spirit, others are drawn to the light that emanates from your life. Your joy testifies to the goodness of God, providing hope and encouragement to those who may be searching for meaning, struggling with despair, or seeking a glimpse of divine love. Let your life be a living witness to the joy that comes from walking with God, and may it inspire others to seek and find that same joy.

A Final Blessing of Joy

My prayer for you, as it is for myself and all persons, is that we continue to grow in joy, finding ourselves closer to God, deepening our experience of His divine grace.

May your days be filled with awareness of God's presence, and may the Holy Spirit guide you into all truth and beauty. May the fruit of the Spirit blossom in you, and may your heart overflow with joy that is radiant, unshakable, and inspiring.

Know that God delights in you, rejoicing over you. As you continue to journey in faith, allow this joy to be your compass, your strength, and the song inside you that creates a rhythm for all the fruit of the Spirit to sing out your life by.

May you find, in every season and every circumstance, that the joy of the Lord truly is your strength. And may you, in your daily walk with Jesus, experience the fullness of joy that comes from being in the presence of God who loves you without measure. Let this joy be your daily meditation, your constant companion, and your eternal hope.

May God Bless You And Keep You

Your Next Fruit...

Peace, as a Fruit of the Spirit is an unshakable tranquility and calmness born of your relationship with Jesus Christ. It is not simply the absence of noise or conflict but a deep-seated stillness that overcomes circumstance while being grounded in the grace of God's sovereignty and love. The peace that passes all understanding gives comfort in the midst of life's storms, anchoring you in the Lord's presence. It fosters harmony with others and cultivates a sense of wholeness. With this peace, God's unwavering care brings a quiet confidence that you will come to know by this 30 day verse, prayer and reflection devotional book. Guiding you into the Fruit of Peace, your heart will open to the presence of Jesus Christ as you receive the grace of God's gentle embrace.

Peace

Your Daily Meditation

Printed in Great Britain
by Amazon

57520602R00056